WHAT IT MEANS TO BE
SERIES

PUBLISHER	Joseph R. DeVarennes
PUBLICATION DIRECTOR	Kenneth H. Pearson
ADVISORS	Roger Aubin
	Robert Furlonger
EDITORIAL MANAGER	Jocelyn Smyth
EDITORS	Ann Martin
	Shelley McGuinness
	Robin Rivers
	Mayta Tannenbaum
ARTISTS	Summer Morse
	Barbara Pileggi
	Steve Pileggi
	Mike Stearns
PRODUCTION MANAGER	Ernest Homewood
PRODUCTION ASSISTANTS	Catherine Gordon
	Kathy Kishimoto
PUBLICATION ADMINISTRATOR	Anna Good

Canadian Cataloguing in Publication Data

Langdon, Anne
   What it means to be—careful

(What it means to be; 17)
ISBN 0-7172-2247-0

1. Prudence — Juvenile literature.
I. Pileggi, Steve.   II. Title.   III. Title: Careful.   IV. Series.

BJ1533.P9L37 1987   j179'.9   C87-095059-2

WHAT IT MEANS TO BE . . .

CAREFUL

Written by
Anne Langdon

Illustrated by
Steve Pileggi

Careful people think things through.

Eva invited Paul back to her house after school one
Tuesday. After they had some juice and a granola
bar, she began to show him around.

"Do you want to see the attic too?" Eva asked.

"Sure!" he cried. "I love attics. I sleep in one,
you know."

There was a window at one end. Paul rushed over
and opened it. "Let's climb out onto the roof," he
suggested. "It would be fun."

Eva poked her head out. She was tempted. It
looked so easy. But she shook her head after a
moment and said, "It looks like fun but it's
dangerous." She pointed to her jungle gym in the
backyard. "You want to climb? Well, let's go into
the backyard. We can climb and swing and there's
even a place to build a fort."

Paul's eyes lit up. "Let's go!"

Being careful means thinking about the
consequences of your actions before you do
something.

Preventing accidents before they happen is a sign of careful thinking.

"It looks like we're in luck," Ms. Barclay said to her grade one class. "The weather forecasters say we'll be getting some warm fall weather this weekend. That's called Indian summer." Looking out at the gray sky, Ryan listened but didn't really believe her.

She turned out to be right though. On Saturday, summer came back for a short visit. Ryan invited Dylan and Jason over to play. They took off their shoes and socks and played tag in the backyard. It felt good to feel the warm grass between their toes.

"Let's play baseball," said Jason after a while.

Ryan ran off to the garage to get his ball and bat. When he returned, he looked around for his two friends but couldn't see them.

"We're up here!" Dylan called. "We're practicing our slides to steal bases." They were running on the deck in their bare feet, trying to slide on the wood.

Ryan remembered the awful sliver he had gotten during the summer from running on the deck. It had hurt a lot. "You could hurt yourselves doing that," he pointed out. "I got a bad sliver in my foot from the deck and had to go to the doctor's. Want to see?" He held up his foot to show them his scar.

"Ah, no thanks," Jason replied. "We get the message." Dylan and Jason hurried down to the lawn to play ball.

Often accidents occur because you're being careless. Remember to be alert and think about what you are doing. You can also keep an eye out for your friends.

It is a good idea to be careful around animals.

Janice was holding Lee's hand and walking him along the sidewalk while Kim watched from the front porch. Lee was in love with the whole world. He tottered around smiling at everything he saw.

Suddenly Kim saw a big, strange dog bounding down the sidewalk toward Janice and Lee. It stopped as it came up to them. Janice kept her distance, but Lee reached out to pat the dog. Kim ran to stop her brother.

"Nice dog," she said gently as she slowly pulled Lee back. "That's a good doggie." Kim took Lee by the hand and walked away.

A few seconds later, a man with a leash came running down the street. "There you are, Fluffy!" he cried. He hooked the leash onto the dog's collar. Then he said, "He's perfectly harmless. But you didn't know that, and you were smart to stay back." He told the children they could pat Fluffy if they wanted to. Lee patted Fluffy and the dog wagged his tail.

If you don't know an animal, it's best to be cautious and not get too close to it.

Do not rely on others to be careful for you.

It was Fall Fair time at school. Everybody was asked to help out any way they could. Some children invented games to play, some brought old toys to sell and others made food. Janice even set up a table at the edge of the schoolyard and told people their fortunes.

As Paul was leafing through an old comic book, he overheard his teacher, Ms. Barclay, talking to Jason's mother.

Ms. Barclay exclaimed, "These roller skates are great. They even have a key to adjust them."

"They've been lying around the house for years," said Jason's mother. "I thought I might be able to sell them."

Paul had never been roller skating before, but he had watched Colette and Kim skating so he figured he could do it too. "Can I try?" he asked. "I know how." That wasn't exactly true, but he wasn't worried. His father was nearby and could help if Paul ran into trouble. But his father was having his fortune read by Janice and wasn't even watching Paul.

Once Paul made the skates smaller using the rusty old key, he slipped them on and fastened the thick leather straps. The skates felt old and stiff but they still worked. Since he knew how to ice skate, he figured that roller skating wouldn't be much different. He was wrong. The wheels rumbled along the walk, going faster and faster.

Soon, Paul was out of control. "Dad!" he yelled. "Help me!"

His father looked up but he was too far away to help. Paul zoomed toward a table full of books. He put his arms over his head, crouched down and hoped for the best. Luckily, he wasn't hurt. The books cushioned his fall. His father rushed over and gently helped Paul up. "Janice really knows what she's talking about."

"What do you mean?" Paul asked.

"She just finished telling me that someone very close to me was going to give me a big surprise," laughed his father. "And that someone turned out to be you!"

_____

Other people may not always be able to rescue you. It's best for you to be careful.

It is important to be careful in and around water.

There was one weekend left before the community pool would be closed for the fall and winter. Saturday was warm and sunny. All the neighborhood kids hurried to the pool, including Mitchell and his stepbrother Jesse. Jesse was ten years old and he was Mitchell's hero. There didn't seem to be anything that Jesse couldn't do.

''Hey, look at this!'' he yelled from the side of the pool. Jesse walked off the edge and into the water as if he hadn't seen it coming. It was funny.

''Get a load of this!'' he shouted, and walked backward into the pool, still pretending to be surprised.

Mitchell wished he could entertain others the way Jesse could. Maybe when Mitchell grew up, he would be able to make people laugh.

"He's pretty funny!" Paul exclaimed.

"He can do stuff like that," said Kim, "because he's older than us."

Meanwhile, Jesse was really clowning it up. Most of the children were giggling and laughing.

"Now, watch this," Jesse called. He climbed the ladder to the high diving board, turning around every once in a while to give them a very serious look. He walked to the end of the board and turned around. He closed his eyes.

"Please follow pool rules," the lifeguard said. "That means no backward diving. I think you're getting a little carried away."

"I'm sorry," Jesse said as he walked back to the ladder. "This time I was going to pretend that I was too chicken to go in anyway."

You can have fun playing and swimming in water. Always follow pool rules and use your common sense to stay safe.

Remember to be careful with other people's belongings.

"Can I try your skateboard?" asked Hannah as she skipped up to Ryan. She was feeling happy and had lots of energy.

"Sure," answered Ryan. "Try it slowly and be careful not to run into anything."

She hopped on his skateboard and tried to make it move by bending her knees and flapping her arms. Nothing happened.

"It's not working," she complained, flipping it over. She kicked the wheels.

"Hey, don't do that!" cried Ryan. He picked it up. "The skateboard is working fine. You just need some practice."

"Hmmph," muttered Hannah.

Mitchell was sitting on his front steps looking at a book. Hannah tiptoed over to him and grabbed his glasses.

"What are you doing?" asked Mitchell crossly.

"Everything looks blurry," she replied as she squinted through his glasses.

"Please give them back," he said.

Hannah slipped them on top of her head. "I won't break them," she muttered.

"Hannah, please give them back," pleaded Mitchell.

She handed him his glasses. There were fingerprints all over the lenses.

"You should treat other people's belongings the same way you want them to treat your things," Mitchell explained quietly. Then he went inside to clean his glasses.

Hannah wandered down the block until she saw huge glistening bubbles floating in the air. Kim was sitting on her lawn blowing bubbles.

"Let me try!" cried Hannah, running over. She reached for the bottle of suds and it spilled.

Kim looked at her without saying a word.

"I'm sorry," mumbled Hannah. "I didn't mean to. I promise to be more careful. Let me help you make some more suds."

"Okay," replied Kim. "Then you can have a turn."

It is best to treat other people's belongings with care and respect.

Always be careful around anything hot.

"How much longer until supper?" Tammy moaned as she followed her mother around the kitchen late one Sunday afternoon.

"A while yet," her mother answered. "It's no use hanging around in here. Go do something—the time will go by faster."

Just as Tammy was about to complain, Colette walked in. "I'm going out to practice my jumps." This week, Colette wanted to be a cheerleader when she grew up. Tammy followed her out the door. Colette began jumping and cheering, and her sister joined in.

Mitchell saw them from his bedroom window and came over to try. "I don't feel as cold when I'm moving," Mitchell panted.

Colette flung her arms in the air, shouting, "Go-o-o-o team!"

Before Tammy knew it, her father was rapping on the living room window, waving them in for dinner. When he saw Mitchell, he opened the window a crack and said, "Mitchell, you're welcome to stay for dinner if you get permission."

Colette began a new cheer about a hero named Mitchell, staying for supper.

Tammy's father was busy keeping the fire in the living room going. As soon as Mitchell was inside, he ran over to the fireplace to put his hands on the screen to get warm.

"Careful!" Colette called.

"That's right," her mother echoed. "It's very hot. I only touch hot things in the oven or on the stove when I have my oven mitts on. They protect my hands from getting burned."

Mitchell stood back a bit enjoying the warmth of the fire.

"Time for supper," Tammy's father called from the kitchen.

They walked to the table with Colette chanting, "Give me an 'S,' give me a 'U' . . ."

You can easily be burned by something that is hot. Remember to keep your distance from fires, stoves and other hot things.

Careful people are alert around cars and traffic.

"We're going to the shopping center to pick up fancy toothpicks," Jason called to Bobby one Saturday morning. "Want to come?"

Bobby wasn't interested in toothpicks but he did feel like going for a ride. He ran inside to ask his dad if it was okay and ran out to say he could go.

On the way, Jason and Janice explained that their parents were having a party that evening. Even though it was for grownups, the children were excited. Some of it rubbed off on Bobby who leaped out of the car as soon as Jason's father had parked it. Bobby started running across the parking lot—straight into the path of a moving car. The car came to a screeching halt. He was really scared. Janice and Jason rushed over to make sure Bobby was okay.

Their father said, "If you ever want to grow up, you have to be more careful around cars."

Bobby's heart was pounding. He would never be that foolish again.

Keep your eyes open and be cautious around cars. Streets and parking lots are not safe places to play.

Being careful means watching where you are going.

"Okay, time to get going," Hannah heard her mother call from the garage. The two of them were going to the airport to pick up a friend of her mother's. She was a professor from Thailand.

"What does she look like?" asked Hannah.

"She has dark hair and she's very tall and her eyes are the same color as yours," her mother said.

Hannah enjoyed riding in the car, watching everything from the window. As they neared the airport, she saw a huge plane with orange and purple stripes come in for a landing. It was gigantic.

After they parked, they entered the busy, noisy airport. There was so much to look at, Hannah couldn't keep her eyes on any one thing for more than a few seconds.

After checking a TV set hanging on a wall, Hannah's mother began to walk down a wide hallway. The more Hannah watched everything around her, the more she found herself banging into things. She bumped into a few people. Some of them snapped at her.

"You should watch where you're going, especially here," her mother said.

"But there's so much to look at," Hannah replied.

Just then a little boy ran right into her, almost knocking her over. An older girl was chasing him.

"See what I mean?" her mother said.

Hannah made sure she didn't bump into anyone else. She stood beside her mother until their visitor arrived.

Pay attention to where you're going at all times so you don't hurt yourself or other people.

Remember to be careful around machines.

"Let's play down in the basement," Joey said to Dylan. The two of them walked down the stairs just as Joey's father was coming up.

The boys were seeing whose fingers were longer when they heard a rumbling from the laundry room. They ran in to investigate, but it was just the washing machine. Dylan noticed a black hose leading into a big sink. He grabbed it, pretending it was a microphone.

"Oh, baby, can't you see I'm drowning in my tears," he began to sing like a rock star. Joey laughed and laughed.

All of a sudden warm, sudsy water began gushing out of the hose and it sprayed all over Dylan. He quickly put the hose back where it belonged. Then he stared down at his soaking wet clothes and started to laugh.

Soon Joey joined in. "Better to drown in your tears than in the laundry room."

Machines are not toys. You should never play with them.

Being careful means being alert around strangers.

Eva arrived at Tammy's front door at the same time as a man she had never seen before. His van was parked in the driveway, and he wore a bright orange shirt and blue pants.

"Hi there," he said to her as he rang the doorbell.

"Hi," Eva answered.

Tammy's mother opened the door and looked surprised to see them standing there together.

"I'm here to fix your television," the man explained.

"Oh yes," she replied. "Come in."

Tammy ran down the stairs to see what was happening. "Who's that man?" she asked Eva after he walked into the recreation room.

"He's going to fix your TV," Eva answered.

Tammy was pleased. She pulled on her sweater and they went outside. She had promised to teach Eva how to tap dance. Tammy began to dance on the sidewalk.

"Think of a song," said Tammy, "just a simple song. Then tap your foot to the beat."

Eva gave it a try. It was fun.

"Now move your arms as well as your feet like this," explained Tammy.

"Wonderful, wonderful!" they heard someone say. They turned around to see a strange man clapping.

"That's what I call real dancing. I know many other talented children. Why don't I take you to meet them?" he suggested, coming nearer.

Tammy thought this was a good idea. She liked meeting people. Maybe she could even learn a new dance. Suddenly Eva grabbed Tammy's hand and began to run to Tammy's house as fast as she could. When they got there, she ran over to Tammy's mother who was working in the garden. Eva explained what had happened.

"You did the right thing," Tammy's mom said. "I'm proud of you for thinking so quickly."

Tammy was confused. "I don't understand."

"You must never go with a stranger," cautioned her mother. "And if someone you don't know asks you to go somewhere, you should run away and tell a grownup you do know."

"I wanted to go with him to meet some new kids," Tammy explained. "I forgot it was wrong to go with strangers. I'll remember next time."

Most strangers do not want to hurt you but a few do. Be cautious of people you don't know and tell an adult if a stranger bothers you.

Careful people put extra time and effort into their work.

The kindergarten class had spent all week painting scenes from fairy tales. There were gigantic dragons, friendly giants and frightening castles. The children taped their paintings at the front of the room.

Mitchell, Tammy and Hannah had worked especially hard on their paintings. They were very pleased with how they had turned out. "Maybe we can even enter an art contest," said Hannah.

Janice walked over to join them. She looked at her scene and then at those her friends had done. There were smudges and a dirty brown footprint at the edge of her painting. She hadn't paid much attention and now she felt ashamed. She took her painting down and walked over to her teacher.

"I'd like to do this again," said Janice quietly. "I can do a much better job if I try harder."

"That sounds like a good idea," Miss Foster replied, smiling.

Taking the time to do your best shows you are a careful worker.

Careful people always think before they do something. They are cautious and alert and they try to avoid accidents and danger whenever possible. Here are some ways to be careful:

- Watch where you are going.
- Stay away from strange animals.
- Do not fool around near the water.
- Never go anywhere with a stranger.
- Be alert around cars and traffic.

Printed and bound in U.S.A.